Praise for Don't Be Weird

"Dawn has done an amazing job articulating the simple things that we all should know when trying to support a friend or family member who has experienced loss. Even as a funeral director of 47 years, at times I find myself unsure of how to help. I wish every guest who walks into a funeral home would read this book before visiting a grieving family."

— *Joe Pray*
Owner and Director, Pray Funeral Home

"Too often, people pull away from those who are grieving because they're afraid of saying or doing the wrong thing. *Don't Be Weird* breaks that barrier in a real and practical way, helping people understand that support isn't about having the perfect words — it's about showing up with presence and intention."

— *Katie Anderson*
Founder, Healing with Katie
Oxford Diploma in Death, Grief and Healing

"Dawn's ability to process her own grief by helping others learn how to support those going through grief is the most generous act of kindness I can imagine. I highly recommend this book to anyone who wants to know how to love their friends well through grief, without being weird."
— *Lisa Kutas*
Chief of Staff, Diocese of Lansing

Don't Be Weird

A Practical Guide to Supporting Your Grieving Friends

Dawn Nowlan

Professor Shea Press/
Charlotte, Michigan

Published by Professor Shea Press
Charlotte, Michigan

ISBN: 979-8-9956892-0-1

First Edition

Printed in the United States of America

Cover design by Dawn Nowlan

For Shea—

The love of my life.

Everything I am, and every word that follows,

is touched by you.

A Note to the Reader

If you picked up this book because someone you love is grieving, first — thank you.

The fact that you are here means you care enough to try, even if you are unsure what to say, afraid of saying the wrong thing, or quietly wondering how to help without making an already painful situation harder.

That matters more than you know.

This book was written from inside grief, not from the outside looking in. It was written in real time, in the months after losing my husband, Shea, when I learned very quickly that most people want to help — they simply do not know how.

Some people showed up beautifully. Some disappeared because they were afraid. Some said exactly the right thing. Some said things so strange I still replay them in disbelief.

And almost all of it came from the same place: love mixed with discomfort.

This book is not about perfection. It is about presence.

It is about helping ordinary people love grieving people well — with honesty, steadiness, humor, and humanity.

You do not need perfect words.

You just need to show up.

If this book helps even one person feel less alone or helps one friend stay when they might otherwise pull away, then it has done exactly what I hoped it would do.

Thank you for being here.

— Dawn

Table of Contents

Introduction

Don't Be Weird: A Practical Guide to Supporting Your Grieving Friends

I never planned on writing a book about widowhood. Especially not at 50. My husband, my sweet Shea, was supposed to be here for decades of adventures, inside jokes, arguments about how much protein you should consume each day, and all the normal, beautiful, messy parts of life. We had a whole future mapped out. And then one random day in July, the map caught fire.

And suddenly - without warning, without a manual, without a "this is what to do when your whole world explodes" checklist - I became a widow.

But this book isn't about *my* grief.

This one is about *yours*: The friends, family, coworkers, neighbors, and good-hearted people who want to help someone who has lost their person… but don't know how. The ones who freeze. The ones who disappear. The ones who mean well but don't want to say the wrong thing and end up saying nothing. The ones who love us, but panic when they see us in the grocery store and suddenly become very interested in the apples.

I started noticing it a couple weeks after the funeral. Then a few months later. Then again. And again. By the **ninth** person - yes, I counted - who said some version of, "I'm so sorry I didn't reach out again… I just didn't know what to say," I had this moment of clarity:

Okay, this is ridiculous. We need a survival guide.

That was the spark.

Not anger. Not bitterness.

Just this very human realization that people are compassionate, but they are scared - scared of saying the wrong thing, scared of making it worse, scared of making us cry, scared of confronting their own mortality.

So, they do nothing.

And that hurts… even though most of them don't mean for it to.

And then there are the moments that stop you in your tracks - the conversations that make you rethink everything. The day after Shea died, many of my dear friends came over. My friend Steve said something that stuck with me like it had been tattooed on my heart:

"Dawn, we were just starting to figure out how to help our friends when their parents die.

We have no idea how to help our friends when our *friends* die."

I swear time froze for a moment.

That's it.

That's the whole thing.

We're 50. We're too young for this and yet here we are. No one taught us how to support our peers when life blindsides them. No one handed us a handbook for how to show up when someone loses their person - not their parent, not their grandparent, but their *partner.* Their person. The one they wake up with and argue with and love with and build an entire existence around.

And the truth is: I don't know what I'm doing either. I'm trying to navigate my whole life without him. That's a different book. (And don't worry – I'll probably write that one too.)

But this book—this one—is for the people who want to love us through the unthinkable. My story comes from losing my person —but grief isn't one-size-fits-all. Whether it's a partner, a parent, a friend, or another kind of loss, the uncertainty of how to show up is something we all share.

There is so much love in this world.

But people don't always know how to give it – especially when grief is involved.

So, this is your permission slip.

Your guide.

Your gentle, humorous nudge.

Your "hey, don't be weird, we're still friends" handbook.

Inside these pages, I'm going to show you:

- What helps
- What doesn't
- What to say
- What to avoid
- How to show up without being intrusive
- How to check in long after everyone else has gone back to normal
- And how to love someone who's grieving in a way that won't feel scary or awkward

This isn't a grief textbook.

It's a human-to-human guide.

A manual written from the inside of a broken heart, for the people standing just outside the door, unsure how to knock.

I'm glad you're here.

Let's walk through it together.

Chapter 1

The Day the World Split in Two

There are days that divide your life into before and after.

Days that change the way light hits a room — how silence sounds, how air moves.

The day Shea died was one of those days.

One moment, I was living the life I knew — the one I built with my soulmate. A life with laughter, inside jokes, shared routines… someone to text when I saw something ridiculous on TikTok, someone who got genuinely excited about my cooking experiments, and someone who encouraged me in everything… except maybe my Amazon Prime account.

And then suddenly… the world shifted.

People say the ground drops out from under you.

That's not true. The ground stays right where it is — you're the one who drops.

You fall into a place you didn't know existed, a place without a map, without rules, without directions.

But here's the part no one prepared me for:

The whole world shifted… and everyone around me shifted too.

It wasn't just my life that cracked — it was how people looked at me, talked to me, approached me, avoided me, whispered near me, hugged me too long, didn't hug me at all, texted once and disappeared, over-texted, under-texted, panicked, froze, acted normal, acted *way* too normal, or acted like I had suddenly become the grieving exhibit at the human zoo.

And honestly?

I can't blame them.

Before this, I didn't know how to act around deep grief either.

Deaths of parents? I understood that script.

Grandparents? Knew that one too.

But a friend losing their spouse in their 40s or 50s?

Losing their forever person?

Their partner in sarcasm, grocery shopping, school events, "what's for dinner," and every mundane thing that quietly builds a life?

We don't have a script for that.

Grief didn't erase who I was.

It just rearranged everything around me.

I think back to the day after Shea died. My friends Steve and Bridget stopped over — as so many dear friends did that day.

Steve said something that stopped me cold — something I had no idea at the time would quietly become a catalyst for this book.

In that moment, I realized how unprepared we are to support one another when the loss isn't theoretical — when it's one of our own.

But not everyone knows what to say.

So, people just… improvise.

And improvisation during tragedy is, well, normally a disaster.

Being thrust into this unwanted afterworld opened my eyes to something important:

Most people want to help. They just don't know how.

They don't want to make us cry, even though we're already crying every day.

They don't want to say the wrong thing, so they say nothing.

They don't want to intrude, so they hover awkwardly from a distance.

They don't want to bring up the loss — as if we aren't living inside it 24/7.

And nearly every single person who avoided me, ghosted me, or froze up said the exact same sentence when I finally ran into them again:

"I didn't reach out because I didn't know what to say."

That was the moment — actually, the ninth time someone said it — that I knew:

Okay.

There needs to be a survival guide.

A guide for the friends.

For the family.

For the coworkers.

For the acquaintances.

For the church parishioners.

For the networking groups.

For anyone who has ever felt paralyzed standing in front of someone whose entire world just shattered.

And yes, there will be heavy parts in these pages — you can't sugarcoat this kind of loss — but there will also be humor, because humor existed deeply in our marriage, and humor is how I survive.

This book isn't about grief theory.

It's not about stages or steps or psychology.

It's about humanity.

It's about connection.

It's about not being weird.

It's about showing up.

It's about loving people through the dark with whatever imperfect words and gestures you have.

If you're reading this, you're already trying — and that's everything.

Welcome to the journey.

We're in this together.

Chapter 2

"I Don't Know What to Say"

(Spoiler: Say Something)

If I had a dollar for every time someone told me, "I just didn't know what to say," I could personally fund the entire grief section at Barnes & Noble.

And honestly? I get it.

Humans panic when life gets raw and unscripted. We like formulas, templates, and autopilot friendliness. We know how to respond to a birthday, a promotion, a new baby, even a colonoscopy.

But sudden loss?

No script.

No rules.

No Hallmark card for "Your world exploded, and I've completely forgotten how my mouth works."

Here's the truth:

It's okay that you don't know what to say.

What hurts far more than you might realize is saying nothing at all.

Silence feels like abandonment.

It feels like disappearing.

It feels like confirmation that the worst thing that ever happened to us is too big for you to handle.

And that's not what any grieving person needs.

Let me say this clearly, gently, lovingly:

Say something. *Anything.* It doesn't have to be perfect — it just has to exist.

Because when someone loses their person, the world gets very quiet very fast. The phone stops buzzing. The doorbell stops ringing. Life goes back to normal for everyone else — except for the one person whose reality has been split in half.

A simple text can feel like a lifeline.

A short message can feel like oxygen.

A tiny check-in can feel like someone turned on a light in a dark room.

And you don't need to deliver a TED Talk.

You don't need to say something profound.

You don't need to fix anything.

You just need to acknowledge reality with kindness.

Why People Freeze

Most people don't stay silent because they don't care.

They stay silent because:

- They're afraid of making you cry
- They're afraid of making themselves cry
- They don't want to "bother" you
- They don't want to be intrusive
- They don't know the right timing
- They're waiting for you to tell them what you need
- They're terrified of saying the wrong thing

But guess what?

You can't make a grieving person sadder. They're already living the worst-case scenario.

You reaching out doesn't "remind" us of anything.

We haven't forgotten.

What you can do is remind us that we're not alone.

And that matters more than you could ever imagine.

What to Say When You Have No Idea What to Say

Let me give you an example from my own life — because it still stands out as one of the most perfect things anyone said to me in those first few weeks.

About two weeks after Shea died, I had to attend a large social event I wanted no part of. I had committed to it long before he passed, and even though my whole body was screaming stay home, I showed up.

The minute I walked in, I felt like I was in a fishbowl — like someone had dimmed the lights and turned me into the evening's special exhibit: *Widow in the Wild.*

Everyone's eyes were on me. Nobody knew what to say. People whispered, looked away, or stared a little too long. It was awful. I felt exposed, fragile, and completely out of place in a room I used to feel comfortable in.

But then I saw two of my friends.

And one of them looked me right in the eye and simply said:

"It's so good to see you, Dawn."

That was it.

No strained pity.

No forced sympathy.

No overly dramatic head tilt.

No panicked, "How are you?" (we'll talk about that later).

Just a warm, genuine acknowledgment that I was there — that I was still a human in the world, and someone was glad to see me.

It was one of the most grounding things anyone said to me that day.

It didn't fix anything.

It didn't need to.

It just made me feel seen.

And when you're grieving, that is everything.

So yes — simple works.

Simple is beautiful.

Simple is safe.

Simple is human.

Say things like:

"It's good to see you."

"I'm really glad you're here."

"You've been on my heart."

These lines are warm without being heavy.

They acknowledge without overwhelming.

They connect without demanding anything in return.

And none of them require you to be Shakespeare.

The Most Powerful Phrase in the Awkward-Moment Toolkit

Let me give you a line that works in literally every situation:

"I don't know what to say, but I didn't want to say nothing."

It's honest.

It's humble.

It's real.

It acknowledges the awkwardness.

It opens the door.

It lands softly.

And it carries zero pressure.

That line alone would've kept more people in my orbit last summer.

The Follow-Up Matters Even More

Most people reach out once, maybe twice.

Then they retreat.

And that's when it hurts.

Because by the time people stop checking in, our world has just gotten quieter — not easier. Months two through six are brutally lonely. The shock wears off, but the absence doesn't.

If you want to help someone who's grieving:

Reach out once in the first few days… and then again. And again. And again.

It doesn't have to be constant.

It doesn't have to be dramatic.

It doesn't have to be deep.

Just consistent.

A ten-second check-in once a week is enough to keep someone tethered.

Grief is isolating — but your consistency is the antidote.

What Not to Say

Don't worry — there's a whole chapter devoted to this. But for now, here's the short list:

Avoid:

"Let me know if you need anything."

"He wouldn't want you to be sad."

"Everything happens for a reason."

"At least he's in a better place."

"You're so strong." (Most of the time, we're just in shock.)

Anything that starts with "At least…"

And please — please, please — do not compare.

For example:

"Well, when I lost…"

This isn't a comparison.

We can talk more about that later, too.

These phrases come from good intentions — but they land like sandpaper on an open wound.

Stick to real.

Simple.

Warm.

Human.

If you remember nothing else

You don't need perfect words.

You don't need to be eloquent.

You don't need to have the answer.

Just show up with your presence, not your perfection.

Say something. Anything.

The fear of saying the wrong thing should never outweigh the power of saying something.

This is how connection survives the unthinkable.

Chapter 3

The One-and-Done Text

Why People Ghost After Tragedy (and How to Come Back)

You know the text I'm talking about.

The one everyone sends in those first 24 hours:

"I can't believe this. I'm so sorry. Please let me know if you need anything."

Then… nothing.

For so many widows and widowers, the day after the funeral is the day after everyone else goes back to normal. The world snaps back into its routine, errands get run, kids get driven, laundry gets folded, dinner gets cooked.

But for us?

Life doesn't snap.

It doesn't return.

It doesn't refill itself.

The shock fades and the silence arrives.

This is the part most people don't understand — not because they don't care, but because they don't know what to do. They think they reached out. They don't want to overwhelm us. They don't want to say the wrong thing… so they fade out quietly, believing they're giving us space.

But from our side, that quiet can feel like being left inside a burning house while everyone else quietly steps away.

Why People Ghost (It's Not What You Think)

People don't go silent because they don't love you.

They go silent because they doubt themselves.

Here are the top reasons I have found people disappear after their first text:

1. They're afraid of making you cry

They think they'll "bring it up" — as if we aren't living with it every second.

And P.S.? I cry every single day. At a whim. Out of nowhere.

So trust me, you're not triggering anything that isn't already right under the surface. You're actually giving us permission to sit in our sadness without feeling like we have to hide it.

2. They don't want to intrude

They assume we're overwhelmed (we are), so they let us "reach out when we're ready" — not realizing we aren't capable of that yet.

You're putting the burden of decision-making onto a griever. And that simply isn't helping.

3. They fear saying the wrong thing

They catastrophize:

"What if I make her upset?"

"What if I say something stupid?"

"What if I'm awkward?"

(For the record, awkward is fine. Silence is not.)

4. They don't know the timeline

They think grief is a short-term crisis — a sprint.

They don't realize it's a long, exhausting, unpredictable marathon that will coexist with us forever.

5. They assume someone else is checking in

Everyone thinks someone else is doing it.

So, no one does.

6. They're grieving too

Sometimes they disappear because their own pain or fear gets in the way.

What the One-and-Done Text Feels Like on Our Side

This part matters.

When you send one supportive text and then disappear, here's how it lands:

• It feels like people saw the "Breaking News" alert and then changed the channel.

• It feels like support was a moment, not a relationship.

• It feels like being loved in a flash, not in a follow-through.

• It feels like friendship shrunk instead of stretched.

Even if the intention was good, the impact can be devastating.

We don't expect people to be perfect.

We don't expect daily attention.

We just need continued presence — not a single digital hug that fades away.

The Good News: You Can Fix It

If you sent that one text and then went quiet, let me tell you something comforting:

It is never too late to come back.

Never.

You didn't ruin the friendship.

You didn't fail permanently.

You didn't miss your one shot.

This isn't a Broadway audition.

This is real life — with real humans who know grief is awkward for everyone.

Here's how to re-enter the conversation with zero weirdness:

How to Come Back After Silence (Scripts Included)

1. Acknowledge It Simply

You don't need a monologue. Just honesty.

- "I realized I went quiet. I didn't know what to say, but I care about you."
- "I should've reached out sooner. I've been thinking about you every day."
- "I'm sorry I disappeared. I was afraid of saying the wrong thing."

Short. Real. Human.

2. Give Permission Not to Respond

This is key.

• "You don't have to reply. Just wanted you to know you're on my heart."

You relieve the pressure completely.

3. Don't Make It About Your Guilt

Be warm, not self-centered.

Avoid:

• "I'm the worst friend."

• "I feel so bad."

• "You must hate me."

We aren't collecting apologies.

We just want connection.

4. Offer Small, Low-Energy Support

Not big commitments. Small ones.

• "I'm headed to the store. Need me to drop off coffee or anything?"

• "Sending you love today. That's all."

• "Here if you want company, silence, or a distraction."

5. Stay Consistent from Here on Out

One message a month is better than one-and-done.

Once a month says:

"I'm still here."

That's all we need.

The Reality No One Talks About

The silence doesn't always come from cowardice.

Sometimes it comes from heartbreak.

Our friends don't know how to support us because no one ever taught them — just like no one taught us how to live through this.

Sudden loss puts everyone in unfamiliar territory — the grieving and the supporting.

But here's the beautiful part:

Awkward love is still love.

Imperfect love is still love.

And love that went quiet can still come back strong.

People just need tools.

And that's why you're reading this.

Chapter 4

Don't Be Weird: Just Treat Me Like Me

If I could print one sentence on a T-shirt, a billboard, a bumper sticker, or the side of every grocery cart in America, it would be this:

Don't. Be. Weird.

I know that sounds blunt, but it comes straight from the trenches. Because here's what happens after you lose your person: the grief is unbearable — but the weirdness of other people is a close runner-up.

Sudden loss doesn't turn us into different people.

It doesn't dissolve our sense of humor.

It doesn't erase our personality.

It doesn't make us breakable crystal that can't be touched.

We're still us.

We're just… hurting.

But people forget this. Or worse — they panic. And when people panic, they act weird.

They speak in hushed tones like they're entering a library.

They tilt their heads so far to the side it looks like their neck is about to snap.

They treat us like we're going to crumble if they make a joke or talk about something normal.

They avoid eye contact.

Or they stare too hard.

Or they freeze completely like someone pressed pause on their face.

And you know what the thing is?

None of that makes grief easier.

It makes us feel more isolated.

It makes us feel like we've become "other," like our identity is now just Widow, capital W.

I didn't stop being Dawn the minute Shea left this world.

I didn't stop loving sarcasm, good wine, travel stories, people-watching, or laughing at inappropriate things.

I didn't suddenly become a somber nun who can only speak in whispers.

I'm me — just me without my person, trying to figure out this new and wildly unwanted chapter.

The Weirdness Spectrum

Let me give you the most common forms of weirdness that pop up after loss. You'll likely recognize a few.

1. The Whisperer

This person lowers their voice to a decibel normally reserved for confessionals or haunted houses.

They mean well, but you want to say,

"It's okay, you can use your regular voice — I'm grieving, not in a library."

2. The Over-Comforter

They hug too long.

They pet your arm.

They say dramatic things like, "I just can't even."

It becomes less comforting and more like being smothered in a blanket of pity.

3. The Avoider

They dodge you in public. They pretend not to see you.

They suddenly become fascinated by the produce section.

You can almost hear the Mission Impossible theme playing as they make their escape.

4. The Panicked Talker

They ramble.

They over-explain.

They keep saying "I'm so sorry" like a broken Siri.

They tell long stories you didn't ask for.

It's like grief made them lose the remote to their own mouth.

5. The Head-Tilt Sympathizer

Head tilts are fine.

But some people tilt like they're trying to balance a heavy thought on their shoulder.

The angle increases with every sentence.

By the end of the conversation, they're practically horizontal.

What We Actually Need

Here's the truth, and it's surprisingly simple:

We need you to show up as YOU.

Not as a grief counselor.

Not as a therapist.

Not as someone delivering their lines in a sad movie.

Just you.

Let us talk normally.

Let us laugh.

Let us curse.

Let us tell a story from before.

Let us talk about our person without you clutching your chest like you're about to faint.

And if we cry?

It's okay.

It's just a Tuesday.

Crying isn't the worst thing that can happen — silence is.

We can cry and still enjoy your company.

We can cry and still laugh ten minutes later.

Grief is weird and layered and unpredictable, but guess what?

We don't break when you treat us like ourselves.

We break when you treat us like we're made of glass.

What "Not Weird" Looks Like

Let me give you examples of what feels normal and grounding — especially in that foggy, early grief phase.

• "Hey Dawn, want to sit together for a bit? No pressure to talk."

• "I saw this meme and thought of you — sending it with zero expectation to reply."

• "I'm running to the store. Need anything?"

• "Let's go for a drive or a walk if you need air."

• "It's good to see you." (One of the most perfect lines ever spoken to me.)

• "You're still you, and I love you."

• "If you want silence, company, or distraction, I'm here for whichever."

You know what all these have in common?

They're natural.

They're human.

They acknowledge the grief without drowning in it.

They honor the relationship we had before this all happened.

Humor Still Exists

Let me be very clear:

Grief does not eliminate laughter.

Shea was the funniest person I ever knew.

Witty, sharp, quick with a comeback, and always ready with the kind of humor that made a room crack open. And being with someone like that for just shy of 30 years? It rubs off on you. It shapes you. It sharpens your own timing and your own edge.

He didn't just make me laugh.

He made me funnier.

He made me see the world in a lighter, quicker, more playful way.

And we raised two kids who are just as witty and sharp as he was.

That humor didn't die with him.

That spark didn't disappear.

I can't — and won't — turn that off.

I need joy.

I need laughter.

I need those moments of lightness to cut through the heaviness of grief, because humor has always been part of how we lived. It's part of our family's DNA.

And humor is not disrespectful to grief.

It's not avoidance.

It's not denial.

Humor is healing.

It's oxygen when the room gets too heavy.

It's the quiet hand on your back that says, "You're still here. Keep going."

It’s the reminder that you can hurt and laugh at the same time — that your humanity didn’t get swallowed by your loss.

So if your grieving friend cracks a joke — don’t panic.

If they laugh — don’t act like it’s a glitch in the matrix.

If they say something honest and dark and sharp — don’t recoil.

Lean into it.

Laugh with them if it feels right.

Let humor have a seat at the table.

Because for many of us, especially those of us who had humor rich in our homes, our marriages, our families…

Laughter isn’t the absence of grief.

It’s proof we’re still alive inside it.

The Bottom Line

We don't need grand gestures.

We don't need perfect words.

We don't need you to tiptoe around us like we're breakable.

We need you to remember who we are.

Talk to us.

Laugh with us.

Sit with us.

Check in without overthinking it.

Be real.

Grief didn't erase our personality — it magnified our need for genuine connection.

Just don't be weird.

Show up as yourself.

Let us be ourselves.

It's really that simple.

Chapter 5

What to Say (and What Not to Say)

A Beginner's Guide to Not Putting Your Foot in Your Mouth During Grief

If you've ever stood in front of a grieving friend and felt your brain short-circuit — like all the words you know in the English language suddenly evaporated — you are not alone.

People panic in these moments.

Their mouth tries to be helpful.

Their brain tries to be wise. I certainly have.

And sometimes the result is… well… terrible.

Not malicious.

Not unloving.

Just terrible.

And listen — I get it. I truly do. No one hands you a script for this stuff. No one teaches you what to say when your friend loses their husband at 50, or their wife at 38, or their partner after 30 years together. You're trying your best in a moment where "best" feels impossible.

This chapter isn't about shaming.

It's about guiding.

Because most hurtful things aren't said out of cruelty — they're said out of panic, discomfort, or misplaced attempts at comfort.

Let's fix that.

WHAT TO SAY

These are the words that land softly.

These are the phrases that comfort without smothering.

These are the lines that helped me breathe during the hardest days of my life.

1. "I'm thinking about you."

Simple. Human. No pressure.

2. "You don't have to respond. Just wanted you to know I care."

This is a gift. The "no response needed" part is everything.

3. "It's so good to see you."

Still one of the most perfect things anyone said to me. No pity. No performance. Just genuine.

4. "If today is heavy, I'm right here."

Acknowledges reality without drowning in it.

5. "This sucks. I'm here in the suckiness with you."

Honest. Real. Not sugar-coated.

6. "I'm not sure what to say, but I didn't want to say nothing."

Possibly the most universally helpful phrase on earth.

7. "Tell me a story about Shea, if you want."

This is huge. Most grieving people want to talk about their person, but they're afraid it will make others uncomfortable.

8. "You're not alone."

A sentence that can change the entire shape of someone's day.

9. "I'm coming by with coffee. If you're not up for talking, I'll just leave it at the door."

Support with boundaries. This feels safe.

10. "Your person mattered."

The acknowledgment widows and widowers crave but rarely hear.

11. "May his memory be a blessing."

A meaningful reminder for the faithful when we need to hear it.

WHAT NOT TO SAY

Now for the tricky part.

These are the phrases that sound comforting but land like a punch to the throat — not because the speakers are bad people, but because the language is tone-deaf to grief.

If you have said any of these, don't spiral.

You're human.

You didn't know.

1. "Let me know if you need anything."

This puts the emotional labor back on the grieving person.

We barely remember to eat. We can't articulate our needs.

2. "He's in a better place."

I understand the intention.

But in the early days? No place is better than here with us.

3. "At least…"

"At least he didn't suffer."

"At least you had so many years together."

Nothing good ever follows "at least."

Grief doesn't need silver linings — it needs support.

4. "You're so strong."

No, we're not.

We're in shock.

Strength isn't what you're seeing — survival is.

5. "Everything happens for a reason."

Please, no. Just… no.

Even if you believe in this deeply, this is not the moment.

6. "God needed another angel."

Even for the most faithful, this one often doesn't land.

7. "I know exactly how you feel."

Even if you've experienced loss, every grief is different.

Instead try: "I've been through something similar, but I know your grief is yours."

8. "Are you dating yet?" / "You're young, you can find love again."

Why is this so common? Truly — why?

9. "He wouldn't want you to be sad."

Grief doesn't follow logic.

And Shea absolutely would want me to feel whatever I need to feel.

10. "Call me if you need anything."

Again — we won't.

Even if we need everything.

11. "When I lost…"

This one is tricky — because it usually comes from a good place.

You're trying to relate.

You're trying to empathize.

You're trying to say, "I've been there too."

But grief is not a competition.

It's not comparable.

And it's not transferable.

When someone is in the middle of fresh loss, this is their moment. Their heartbreak. Their story.

As hard as it is not to compare, sharing your experience right then often shifts the focus — even unintentionally — from them to you.

Instead of feeling supported, the grieving person can feel unseen.

That doesn't mean your loss doesn't matter. It does.

It just means this moment belongs to them.

If you truly want to empathize, try this instead:

"I've been through something painful too, but I know this is your grief. I'm here to listen."

Let their story stay centered.

There will be time for yours later.

THE GRIEF SAFE-ZONE PHRASES

If you are at a total loss for words, these are your fail-safe options.

You cannot go wrong with these:

- "I love you."
- "I'm here."
- "You're not alone."
- "Take your time. I'm not going anywhere."
- "I'm walking beside you through this."

They're short.

They're grounded.

They're human.

They don't require a grief degree.

THE SECRET SAUCE: SAY THEIR NAME

One of the most meaningful things you can do?

Say their person's name.

It's astonishing how many people avoid it, like the name itself is radioactive.

But hearing "Shea" is like hearing a piece of home.

It's a reminder that he existed, that he mattered, that his life didn't evaporate the moment his heartbeat stopped.

If you want to comfort a grieving friend, you can never go wrong with sentences like:

- "I was thinking about Shea today."
- "Shea was such a light."
- "Shea would've loved this story."
- "One thing I loved about Shea was…"
- "Shea would have absolutely roasted you for saying that."

And here's the important part:

It's not painful to hear his name.

What's painful is when no one says it.

THE BOTTOM LINE

People don't need perfect words.

They need presence.

They need honesty.

They need you.

And the best thing you can do — the most supportive, compassionate, grounded thing — is to speak softly, simply, and sincerely.

Nothing fancy.

Nothing profound.

Nothing "wise."

Just words spoken from the heart to remind your grieving friend that you see them, you honor their person, and you're walking beside them.

That's it.

That's enough.

That's everything.

Chapter 6

Showing Up Without Taking Over

There is an art to supporting someone who is grieving. Not a science — an art. And like all art, some people naturally have the instinct… and others need a little coaching.

On one end of the spectrum, you have the people who do nothing.

On the other end, you have the people who do everything — including things you never asked for, never wanted, and never agreed to.

Both extremes come from the same place: love mixed with fear.

But let's be honest — both extremes can make the grieving person feel worse.

So, what does the middle look like?

What does healthy, grounded, respectful support actually feel like?

This chapter is your guide to that sweet spot:

Showing up… without taking over.

---

1. The Difference Between Helpful and Overwhelming

Grief is exhausting.

Not "I stayed up too late last night" exhausting — but "my brain is running 73 tabs at once and my heart is carrying 600 pounds of emotion" exhausting.

So when people swoop in with big, intense, hyper-enthusiastic offers:

- "I'll clean your whole house!"
- "I'll take over your calendar!"
- "Let me manage everything!"

…it can feel like pressure. Or pity. Or like they've decided we're incapable of functioning.

Here's the truth:

We can function.

We just can't function at full capacity.

We don't need someone to run our entire life.

We need someone to support our life.

The difference is huge.

---

2. Offer Support in Small, Actionable Ways

The best offers are small, simple, and specific.

Try things like:

• "I'm at the store. Want milk, coffee, or dog treats?"

• "I'm free Thursday — want company, silence, or a ride somewhere?"

• "Can I grab the kids from practice for you this week?"

• "Want me to handle dinner on Friday?"

• "Need help opening mail or going through paperwork?"

These aren't overwhelming.

They're bite-sized support that says:

"I'm here. I see you. I'm not taking your life over — just lightening the load."

---

3. Respect Their Boundaries (Even If They Change Every Hour)

Grief is unpredictable.

Your grieving friend may want company at 2 p.m.

Then want silence at 2:07 p.m.

Then want to talk at 2:15 p.m.

Then want to cry into their sleeve by 2:20.

This is normal.

Support-people sometimes take shifting boundaries personally.

Don't.

If your friend cancels…

If they change plans…

If they say "not today"…

If they go quiet…

It's not you.

It's grief.

The best thing you can say is:

- "No worries at all — I'm here whenever you want."
- "No pressure. Take your time."
- "Whatever you need today is okay."

This creates emotional safety — a gift most people don't realize grieving people desperately need.

---

4. Don't Be the Fixer

One of the hardest things for people to accept is this:

You cannot fix it.

You cannot fix the loss.
You cannot fix the pain.
You cannot fix their world.

Trying to rescue them from grief doesn't help.
Trying to fast-track their healing doesn't help.
Offering "solutions" doesn't help.

What helps?

• Listening.

• Sitting.

• Caring.

• Being patient.

• Letting them feel what they feel.

Your presence is the support.

Not your solutions.

---

5. Be Proactive — But Not Controlling

There's a balance between disappearing and micromanaging.

Healthy support looks like:

• Proactively checking in

• Offering help without insisting

• Being consistent without smothering

• Showing up without overshadowing

• Caring without controlling

It sounds like:

• "I'm going to stop by with soup — want me to leave it on the porch?"

• "Want company for a bit, or should I give you space tonight?"

• "I'm going for a walk if you want to join."

See the difference?

It's supportive, not demanding.

---

6. Hold Space Without Filling It

This is subtle but important.

Holding space means:

• Being present

- Being calm
- Letting the grieving person lead the conversation
- Not needing to lift the mood
- Allowing silence without panic

You don't need to fill the quiet.

You don't need to cheer them up.

You don't need to redirect the sadness.

Sometimes the most healing moments happen in shared silence — the kind where someone sits next to you, doesn't flinch when you cry, and doesn't sprint for the metaphorical exit when the conversation gets real.

Those are the people who help us the most.

---

7. Don't Make Everything About the Loss

This one surprises people.

Grief is real and huge — but it's not the only thing happening in our lives.

Please don't treat every interaction like a therapy session.

It's perfectly okay to talk about:

- What's going on in your world
- Something funny that happened
- A show you watched
- A new restaurant
- Normal life things

We need both:

Space for the grief
AND space for being human.

You don't have to tiptoe.
You don't have to speak in hushed tones.
You don't have to bring up the loss every time.

Let life be life.

Let us be us.

The Bottom Line: Show Up, Don't Take Over

Support doesn't have to be dramatic.

It doesn't have to be loud.

It doesn't have to be all-encompassing.

It just has to be steady, respectful, simple, and human.

Show up.

Check in.

Offer small, meaningful help.

Respect boundaries.

Stay consistent.

Let them lead.

Let them feel.

Let them laugh.

Let them cry.

Let them breathe.

Let them be.

You don't need to hold their whole world.

Just their hand through it.

Chapter 7

The Calendar Doesn't Care

Holidays, Anniversaries, and the Dates That Hit Harder Than Expected

There is something no one warns you about when someone dies:

The calendar keeps moving.

It doesn't slow down.

It doesn't pause out of respect.

It doesn't circle the hard days in red and whisper, "Are you ready?"

It just keeps flipping.

And every flip can feel like a landmine.

The first holiday.

The first birthday.

The first anniversary.

The first random Tuesday that meant something only the two of you understood.

And sometimes — it's not even the "big" dates.

For me, Shea died on July 16th.

So every 16th of the month, I feel it.

Two months without him.

Five months without him.

Seven months without him.

They're not official anniversaries. They're not years.

But they're still deathiversaries.

And those days can feel daunting in a way that's hard to explain to someone who hasn't lived it. The body remembers. The mind counts. The heart replays.

If you know the date your friend lost their person — the three-month mark, the six-month mark, even just the monthly rhythm — those quiet check-ins matter more than you realize.

The First Big Holiday

The first holiday without your person is disorienting.

But here's something I learned:

Not all holidays hit equally.

Shea died in July.

We made it through Labor Day.

We made it through Halloween.

But Thanksgiving?

That one broke me.

He loved Thanksgiving.

Loved the food, the gathering, the noise, the ritual of it.

The empty chair was deafening.

And then Christmas came.

And Christmas was too much.

I couldn't wake up on Christmas morning in our house. I couldn't pretend traditions were intact when the center of them was gone. So the kids and I left town. We escaped. We did something different.

Maybe next year will look different. But this year? Survival was enough.

If your grieving friend is approaching a first big holiday, say something.

Not something dramatic. Just something aware.

- "I know Thanksgiving might feel different this year."
- "I'm thinking about you heading into Christmas."
- "Want to change it up this year?"
- "How are you feeling about the holiday?"

You acknowledging the shift doesn't make it worse.

Silence does.

New Year's: The Hardest Holiday of All

People think Christmas is the worst.

But for many grieving people?

New Year's Eve is the monster.

Because New Year's is about:

- Time passing
- Moving forward
- Leaving one year and entering another
- Realizing your person will not be part of the year ahead

And for someone whose life exploded within the last twelve months, that countdown is brutal.

Midnight doesn't feel hopeful.

It feels final.

It feels like the world is cheering for a future you didn't ask for.

For me, the realization hit right after Christmas. The buildup to Christmas had been so heavy that I hadn't even thought ahead to January.

And then it struck me:

I was about to enter a year where I would no longer say,

"My husband died this year."

It would become, "My husband died last year."

I was about to move into a calendar year that Shea would never be part of.

That shift — that linguistic shift — felt like another loss.

It's still hard to write, let alone fathom. And I can almost guarantee this is something every widow and widower faces: the first time the year rolls over and permanence settles in differently.

The future doesn't just look different.

It looks absent.

So if your grieving friend is staring down New Year's Eve, support them gently.

Say things like:

• "You made it through the hardest year of your life. I'm proud of you."

• "If you want company tonight, I'm here."

• "If you want to ignore New Year's completely, that's okay too."

• "If you want to toast to Shea tonight, say the word."

And please — avoid the motivational slogans.

Don't say:

• "Fresh start!"

• "New year, new chapter!"

• "This year will be better!"

• "Time to move forward!"

Grief doesn't flip with the calendar.

Forward isn't a switch.

Let them decide how to exist in that moment.

Quietly. Loudly. Celebrating. Avoiding. Crying. Sleeping. Crushing a pint of Häagen-Dazs.

Just let them decide.

Joy Doesn't Wait for Grief to Finish

Here's something else the calendar doesn't care about:

Other people's joy keeps happening.

On Labor Day weekend, just weeks after Shea died, his oldest brother got married in Seattle.

Shea was supposed to be there.

I wasn't planning to go — I had already traveled a lot that year — but the day after the funeral, I felt this tug on my heart.

I needed to represent. So I went. And it was harder than I expected.

Being at a wedding so soon after losing your spouse is disorienting. By September 1st, I had already attended two weddings. The irony wasn't lost on me — Shea passed July 16th, and I was standing at celebrations of lifelong love just weeks later.

It was painful. And it was beautiful.

I was so happy to see Shawn happy. I know Shea would have been too.

And that's the strange, complicated truth about grief:

Love, joy, and sorrow don't take turns anymore. They live braided together. Fused together.

You can cry in the car and toast at the reception.

You can ache for what you lost and celebrate someone else's beginning. You can miss your person fiercely and still clap when someone says, "I do."

One doesn't cancel out the other. They coexist now.

If your grieving friend attends your milestone event — wedding, graduation, baby shower, birthday — understand that it likely took more emotional courage than you realize.

They are showing up in layers.

Acknowledge that quietly.

- "Thank you for being here."
- "I know this might feel complicated."

That awareness means everything.

Birthdays & Death Days

There are two dates that carry a unique kind of weight:

Their birthday.

And the anniversary of their death.

We just had Shea's first birthday without him.

The buildup was torture.

The week leading up? Torture.

The quiet counting down? Torture.

The replaying of memories? Torture.

By the time Sunday arrived, I was already emotionally wrung out.

We cried a lot that day — especially leading up to the gathering.

The day started with dear friends praying the rosary at his final resting place. I don't even know how many were there, but knowing they were there — praying for Shea, praying for us, loving him in such a meaningful way — brought me profound comfort.

There was something deeply grounding about that kind of love: quiet, faithful, present, asking nothing in return. Before the family arrived, before the tears and the toast and all the emotions the day would carry, that simple act reminded me that grief is heavy, but love still keeps showing up.

But then something beautiful happened.

Shea's siblings who live in-state and their children came over. One of his cousins and their spouse came too. One of my best friends came over as well. We started by toasting him at his gravesite. Then we came back to the house and ate all of his favorite foods.

The day itself was good.

Tender.

Sad.

Full.

Hard.

But good.

The buildup was worse than the day.

And that's something people don't talk about enough.

If you want to show up well, don't just check in on the day itself.

Check in before.

- "I know his birthday is coming up. I'm thinking about you this week."
- "Next week might be heavy. I'm here."

That kind of foresight feels like love.

The World Forgets Faster Than We Do

Another hard truth?

The world moves on faster than the grieving person does.

The first holiday season is marked.

The first birthday is acknowledged.

But by month eight?

By month eleven?

People assume you're "doing better."

Grief doesn't run on a social timeline.

It doesn't fade neatly with the calendar year.

And remembering those dates — even the quiet ones — says:

"I haven't forgotten."

"Your person still matters."

"You still matter."

Let Them Do It Their Way

Some grieving people want to gather.

Some want solitude.

Some want distraction.

Some want to toast at a gravesite and then eat their person's favorite foods.

Some want to disappear entirely.

There is no correct way to grieve a holiday.

Don't pressure them to "keep traditions alive."

Don't insist they attend everything.

Don't force cheerfulness.

Ask.

Offer.

Follow their lead.

What This Really Comes Down To: Mark the Date

You don't have to fix the sadness.

You don't have to orchestrate healing.

You don't have to know the perfect words.

Just mark the date.

Say their name.

Send the text.

Acknowledge the shift.

Because the calendar may not care.

But you can.

Chapter 8

When the Griever Pulls Away

And How to Love Someone Who's Retreating into Their Pain

There's something else no one talks about enough:

Sometimes the grieving person goes quiet.

Sometimes we stop responding.

Sometimes we cancel plans.

Sometimes we pull back.

Sometimes we disappear into our own silence.

And from the outside, it can look like:

"She doesn't want help."

"He's isolating."

"They're pushing people away."

But most of the time?

We're not rejecting you.

We're overwhelmed.

Grief Shrinks Your Capacity

Grief doesn't just hurt.

It shrinks your emotional bandwidth.

Texting back feels exhausting.

Making decisions feels impossible.

Small talk feels absurd.

Plans feel like pressure — even when they're loving plans.

There were moments when I didn't even realize I was pulling

away.

I would see a text come in and think,

"I just don't have it in me."

Not because I didn't love the person.

Not because I wasn't grateful.

Not because I didn't care.

I just didn't have the emotional bandwidth.

And sometimes, if I'm being honest, it felt like:

What's the point?

There is a neurological shift that happens in grief. It's more than widow fog. Your whole system is recalibrating. Your brain, your nervous system, your emotions, your body — everything is trying to rewire itself around a new reality.

You are not just missing someone.

You are learning how to exist without them.

For me, Shea and I were together since I was 20 years old.

That's my entire adult life.

I don't know *how* to adult without him.

I'm figuring that out in real time.

So when someone would ask, "Want to grab dinner?" or "Want to hang out?" in those early months, it wasn't that I didn't want to see them.

It was that it felt like too much.

Grief makes even simple decisions feel monumental.

The Vortex Is Real

There is a vortex in grief.

It pulls you toward isolation.

Toward sweatpants.

Toward sitting in your sadness because it's easier than mobilizing.

And as depressing as that sounds, it's honest.

It is easier to stay home.

It is easier to not respond.

It is easier to avoid the energy it takes to show up.

I caught myself getting pulled into that vortex.

And I had a choice.

I knew how loved I was.

I knew how many people were pouring into me.

And I didn't want to become unreachable.

So sometimes the bravest thing I did was say yes.

And here's the surprising part:

Once I went, I usually had a good time.

Did I cry?

Yes.

Did I still miss him?

Of course.

But it was good to not cook.

Good to sit with friends.

Good to drink a glass of wine (or two).

Good to be with people who cared about me without making everything heavy.

Sometimes the hardest part isn't going.

It's saying yes.

———

If Your Grieving Friend Goes Quiet

If someone you love starts pulling away, remember:

It's probably not about you.

They are navigating a full-body, full-brain rewiring process.

Instead of retreating yourself, try:

• "No pressure to reply — just thinking of you."

• "Still here."

• "Want me to keep inviting you even if you say no sometimes?"

That last one? Gold.

Because sometimes we want to be invited.

Even if we're not ready yet.

Consistency without pressure is the sweet spot.

Don't Say, "Well, I Tried."

Grief is not a one-attempt situation.

If someone doesn't respond, it doesn't mean they don't need you.

It means they're tired.

Stay steady.

Not invasive.

Not relentless.

Just steady.

For the Griever Reading This

If you're the one who's been pulling away:

You're not failing at friendship.

You're not ungrateful.

You're not cold.

You are exhausted.

But here's a gentle encouragement:

Let one or two safe people stay close.

Say yes occasionally.

Even if it feels heavy at first.

Connection is part of the healing — even when it requires effort.

You don't have to be social.

You don't have to perform.

You don't have to explain.

But don't let the vortex take everything.

The Bottom Line

Grief changes behavior.

Pulling away doesn't mean someone stopped loving you.

It means they're surviving something enormous.

Support in this season looks like:

Consistency without pressure.

Invitation without obligation.

Presence without demand.

And sometimes, the most powerful thing you can do — on either side of grief — is simply keep showing up.

Chapter 9

When You Don't Know the Griever That Well

Coworkers, Acquaintances, Neighbors, Church Members, and Everyone in the "We Care but We're Not Sure How" Category

Not everyone who wants to show up for a grieving person is a best friend.

Sometimes the people who want to help the most are the ones who don't know the grieving partner very well — or at all. They may know of them. They may follow them on social media. They may have met them a handful of times at events. They may be part of the same workplace, neighborhood, church community, or volunteer group.

And because they don't have a deep relationship, these people often do… nothing.

Not because they don't care — but because they don't want to overstep.

But here's the truth:

You don't need a deep relationship to offer real comfort.

You just need kindness — and a little confidence.

This chapter is for the people in that space: the ones who care but aren't sure if it's their place.

---

1. Acknowledge the Loss — Don't Ignore It

Acquaintances often avoid mentioning the loss because they assume:

"It's not my place."

"They probably don't want to talk about it."

"They have close friends for that."

"It might be awkward."

But ignoring the loss is almost always worse.

You don't need a long conversation.

You don't need to dive into feelings.

You don't need to deliver wisdom.

A simple acknowledgement works beautifully.

Examples:

- "I'm so sorry for your loss."
- "I've been thinking about you."
- "My heart goes out to you."
- "You and your family have been on my mind."
- "I'm holding you in prayer."

These are human phrases — not intrusive ones.

---

2. Keep It Simple, Gentle, and Low-Pressure

When you're not close, the safest approach is simple consistency.

Things like:

- Sending a card
- Dropping off a small meal
- Messaging once in a while just to say "Thinking of you today"
- Offering small, specific help like "I'm at the store — need milk?"
- Smiling warmly when you see them instead of panicking or looking away
- Saying a genuine "It's good to see you"

You don't need intimacy to offer kindness.

You just need sincerity.

---

3. Don't Overestimate How Much You Need to Do

Acquaintances sometimes worry:

"If I text, they'll think I'm trying too hard."

"If I bring food, that's something only close friends do."

"If I check in, it might seem weird."

Let me clarify something:

Grief does not have tiers.

Support isn't reserved for the "inner circle."

You don't need permission to be kind.

You don't need closeness to be compassionate.

You don't need history to be human.

Even small gestures from acquaintances can feel enormous.

---

4. Respect the Boundaries of the Relationship

Being supportive does not mean crossing lines.

If you weren't close before the loss:

- Don't expect deep conversations
- Don't pry for details
- Don't ask how they're "really doing"
- Don't expect emotional intimacy in return
- Don't force a new closeness they didn't initiate

Your role is simple:

Be steady.

Be kind.

Stay in your lane.

Acquaintance support is quiet support — and it matters.

---

5. How to Show Up in Public or Group Settings

Many acquaintances panic when they run into a grieving person in public — at work, at church, or at a community event.

Here's what to do:

Make eye contact.

Smile genuinely.

Say "It's good to see you."

Offer a brief hug if appropriate.

Keep the interaction natural.

Don't freeze.

Don't avoid them.

Don't whisper.

Don't treat them like a ghost.

Remember:

Your normal presence feels far safer than your avoidance.

---

6. The Perfect Acquaintance Message (Feel Free to Borrow This)

For people who aren't sure if it's "their place," here's a message that works in almost every situation:

"We haven't talked much, but I just wanted to say I'm so sorry for your loss.

You don't need to respond — I just want you to know I'm thinking about you."

Pressure-free.

Supportive.

Kind.

Respectful.

You can't go wrong with that.

---

7. When You Want to Do More — But Don't Want to Overstep

If you feel moved to help more, but you're not sure how, try something soft and optional, but not too vague:

- "If I can ever drop off a meal, I'd be honored."
- "If you ever need someone to run an errand, I'm close by."
- "If you need an extra set of hands with anything house-related, I'm here."
- "If you want company for a walk, I'm around."

Just remember to include the most important phrase:

"No pressure at all."

---

8. Acquaintance Support Often Matters More Than You Realize

Here's the secret grieving people rarely say out loud:

Sometimes acquaintances show up in ways close friends don't.

Not because close friends don't care — but because acquaintances aren't as afraid of getting it wrong.

Acquaintances often:

Check in gently.

Send supportive messages.

Don't overthink every word.

Don't disappear out of fear.

Don't expect emotional labor.

They simply offer kindness.

Sometimes it's the woman from yoga, the guy from the office, or the neighbor down the street who quietly becomes one of the most consistent sources of compassion.

Those small gestures matter.

A lot.

---

9. Kindness Sometimes Comes from Unexpected Places

One of the most surprising parts of grief is discovering how many lives your person touched — including people you've never even met.

After Shea died, I received gifts and messages from people I didn't know personally, but who loved him in their own way. Some were friends of friends. Some had crossed paths with him through work or community. Some had simply heard about his life and wanted to show support.

There were generous gifts, including financial support that helped our family navigate the immediate weeks when I had to step away from work to make important decisions. Those acts of generosity lifted a burden I didn't even have the strength to name at the time.

I also received something deeply meaningful in my faith: people arranged for Catholic Masses to be offered for Shea's soul. To many people that might sound like a small gesture, but to me it meant more than I can fully explain. It was a profound act of love and prayer that I will always carry with gratitude.

And then there were the people who came to his viewing — strangers to me, but not to him.

They stood in front of me and told me stories about how Shea had made them laugh, how he had helped them, how he had made them feel seen or welcome or encouraged. These were moments of his life I had never witnessed.

Those stories were gifts.

Treasures.

Little pieces of my husband's impact in the world that I now get to carry forward for our children.

All because someone who didn't know me well decided to show up anyway.

That kind of kindness is never small.

What Matters Most

You don't need to be a best friend to be a good friend.

You don't need years of history to offer humanity.

You don't need closeness to offer comfort.

If you care, show it — simply, softly, steadily.

Because grief belongs to the grieving person…

but support belongs to all of us.

Chapter 10

The Long Haul

Showing Up at Month 4, Month 7, Month 12 and Year 2

Here's another thing nobody tells you about grief:

It often gets harder right when people think it should be getting easier.

In the beginning, support is everywhere.

The texts.

The meals.

The flowers.

The cards.

The hugs.

The messages.

The people who say, *"Call me any time."*

But eventually the casseroles stop.

The texts slow down.

Life goes back to normal for everyone else.

Meanwhile, the grieving person's heart is still on fire.

This chapter is for the friends who want to understand what happens after the funeral, after the shock, after the first few months — and how to show up in a way that actually matches the grieving person's reality.

Month 4: When the Heaviness of Grief Begins

By month four, the shock starts to fade.

And what's underneath the shock?

Reality.

The forever-ness.

The weight of the empty bed.

The silent house.

The future that was supposed to be.

This is often when:

- The fog lifts just enough for the pain to hit harder
- People start expecting "improvement"
- The grieving person feels like the world has moved on
- Friends stop checking in
- Loneliness grows larger
- Random moments become emotional landmines
- The second wave of grief hits like a tsunami

Month four is often the first time the grieving person feels the loss fully — and painfully.

This is when your consistency matters more than ever, even if you think things are "getting better."

Try messages like:

- "I know it's been a few months. I'm still here."
- "Thinking of you today — no need to reply."
- "You're not forgotten."

• "Just checking in on you."

Small check-ins can make a huge difference.

Month 7: The Silent Middle Ground

Month seven is the forgotten season of grief.

Not early.
Not late.

Too far from the loss for people to remember.
Too close for the grieving person to feel healed.

Right in the middle of nowhere.

Month seven often looks like:

• Going through the motions
• Smiling on the outside

- Breaking on the inside
- Learning new routines
- Avoiding the reality of certain milestones
- Living in what I call **functional grief**

Functional grief is one of the most misunderstood phases of loss.

People may say things like:

"Wow, you seem to be doing so much better."

But month seven is often when the grieving person feels the most alone.

Because they've learned how to function.

But they haven't learned how to live again yet.

Support during this season might look like:

- "Hey, just checking in — how's your heart today?"
- "No agenda, just care."

- "You crossed my mind today."
- "I'm proud of you for getting through each day."

Month 12: The One-Year Trigger

People often assume the one-year mark brings closure.

It doesn't.

It can feel like reopening the original wound — but this time with full awareness of what has been lost.

The entire month leading up to the anniversary can feel heavy, surreal, and disorienting.

Every detail from the previous year comes rushing back:

Where we were.

What we were doing.

The hours before.

The moment everything changed.

The blur that followed.

The disbelief.

The chaos.

The heartbreak.

The one-year anniversary isn't just a date.

It's a full-body memory.

And here's the part many people don't realize:

Most people don't check in around this time because they assume you're "doing better now."

But the grieving person will never forget that date — not once, not ever.

Your acknowledgment will feel like love.

Try messages like:

- "Holding you close today."
- "Thinking of Shea and thinking of you."

- "I remember what today means. I'm here."
- "You're not walking through this day alone."

These messages matter more than you know.

Year 2: The Quietest Year of All

Year two is where grief becomes invisible to almost everyone except the grieving person.

By now:

- The shock is gone
- The early support has faded
- People assume life has returned to normal
- The world has moved on

But the grieving person still carries the absence every single day.

Many widows and widowers describe year one as living inside a kind of **widow fog**. The pain is real — overwhelming, even — but the shock and numbness can act like a protective shield.

Almost like emotional Novocaine.

You're surviving.

Your brain is still trying to process something that doesn't make sense yet.

By year two, that fog often lifts.

And when it does, the reality of the loss can land in an entirely different way.

You're no longer just surviving moment to moment.

You're living with clarity.

Clarity that this is real.

Clarity that this is permanent.

Clarity that this is the life now.

Many grieving people describe year two as grief **without Novocaine**.

It's when the quiet moments start to carry a different weight.

A ringtone that sounds like the one your person used.

A song that played in the car.

A familiar smell or routine.

For a split second, your brain forgets.

You feel a tiny flutter of recognition — a brief spark of hope — before reality catches up and reminds you they will never call again.

Those moments are fleeting, but they can hurt in ways that are difficult to explain.

I haven't reached year two yet myself as I write this.

But I'm approaching it.

And if I'm honest, I dread it.

Not because I think I won't survive it — I know I will.

But because I know the fog that helped cushion the first year will lift, and the permanence of this loss will come into even sharper focus.

It's the moment when the quiet realization settles in:

This is forever now.

Year two often feels like:

Acceptance and heartbreak living side by side.

Moments of joy mixed with deep sadness.

Learning how to live again — while still missing them fiercely.

Holidays still complicated.
Anniversaries still heavy.
A quiet, persistent loneliness.

Year two is often when people stop asking how you're doing — which ironically is when grief becomes more realistic, more settled, and sometimes more painful.

Support during this time might look like:

- "Hey, I know it's been awhile — just checking in."
- "I think of Shea often."
- "Hope today is gentle on you."
- "Sending you love today."

Consistency doesn't need to be loud.

It just needs to exist.

Why People Disappear — Again

Friends sometimes disappear during the long haul because:

- They assume time heals everything
- They think checking in might "bring it up"
- They don't want to pry
- They believe you're doing better
- They forget that grief doesn't follow a calendar

And again, it's rarely malicious.

It's simply ignorance — the innocent, human kind.

This chapter is your chance to help people understand how to stay.

The Simple Long-Haul Formula

If you want to support someone through long-term grief:

Keep showing up.

Not every day.

Not every week.

Not dramatically.

Just steadily.

Once a month is enough.

Twice a month is beautiful.

Major milestones? Essential.

Your message doesn't need poetry.

It doesn't need depth.

It doesn't need perfect timing.

It just needs to be real.

"Thinking of you today."

"You crossed my mind."

"Hope your day has a soft moment in it."

"Still here."

Support isn't measured in intensity.

It's measured in **consistency**.

Here's the Truth

Grief doesn't follow a schedule.

There is no deadline.

No finish line.

No moment when it magically stops hurting.

But the people who keep showing up —

At month four,

Month seven,

Month twelve,

Year two,

And beyond —

Those are the people who help the grieving heart slowly rebuild its rhythm.

You don't need to fix anything.

You don't need to understand everything.

You just need to stay.

Because grief is long —

and love is longer.

Chapter 11

Learning to Live in the After

When Grief and Life Begin Sharing the Same Space

If you had asked me before Shea died what grief looked like, I probably would have imagined something tidy.

Sadness.

Healing.

Acceptance.

Moving forward.

A straight line.

But grief is not tidy.

Grief is not linear.

Grief is not a checklist you complete and move on from.

Grief is something you learn to carry while continuing to live.

And eventually — slowly, awkwardly, at times painfully — life begins to grow around the grief.

This chapter isn't about "getting over" loss.

That phrase doesn't exist in real life.

This chapter is about something quieter and far more honest:

Learning how to live in the after.

Life Starts Tapping on Your Shoulder Again

One of the strangest parts of grief is the moment when normal life begins creeping back in.

At first it feels wrong.

You laugh at something and immediately feel guilty.

You enjoy a conversation and think,

How can I feel joy when the worst thing imaginable happened?

You catch yourself having a good day and feel almost disloyal.

But here's something grieving people slowly learn:

Joy and grief are not enemies.

They can sit in the same room.

You can laugh and still miss them.

You can feel peace and still feel heartbreak.

You can have moments of happiness and still carry enormous loss.

Joy doesn't erase love.

And love doesn't disappear when someone dies.

The First Time You Feel Like Yourself Again

There will be a moment — maybe months in, maybe years — when something unexpected happens.

You'll laugh.

Not the polite smile you've been giving people when you're exhausted.

Not the "I'm trying to look okay" laugh.

The real one.

The one that bubbles up before you even think about it.

And when it happens, you might pause.

Because for a second, you felt like yourself again.

That moment can feel confusing.

Beautiful.

Painful.

Hopeful.

All at once.

Because you realize two things simultaneously:

You are still capable of joy.

And you wish they were there to see it.

Humor Still Has a Seat at the Table

Something else I've realized about grief is that humor doesn't disappear.

At least not for people like us.

Shea and I had a very specific brand of humor in our house — a lot of it inappropriate, immature, a little dark, and absolutely hilarious to us. The kind of humor that made other people raise an eyebrow while we were high-pitched cry- laughing.

Shea had a habit of saying something wildly inappropriate just to get a reaction out of people. Someone would gasp, someone would shake their head, and then he would look straight at me — completely deadpan — and say, *"I'll be good."*

Which, of course, only made me laugh harder.

And then there were his siblings.

Individually, they are perfectly reasonable, lovely people.

Put them together, though, and it's like a full set of Power Rangers assembling. Suddenly the room is chaos — late nights, too much wine, movie quotes, ridiculous stories — and the evening would inevitably end with Shea announcing, *"It's time for a refresher."*

That was our life. It was wonderful.

And I can't just turn that part of it off now.

So yes, sometimes my healing looks like doom-scrolling through social media and watching wildly inappropriate reels. Sometimes it looks like sending those reels to my in-laws or my kids just to see who reacts first.

Sometimes laughter comes from the most ridiculous places.

And you know what?

That's okay.

Humor doesn't dishonor the person we lost.

It honors the life we shared with them.

If anything, I think Shea would be the first one laughing at— and probably the first one sending— the inappropriate reel.

Grief doesn't erase your personality.

It doesn't erase your inside jokes.

It doesn't erase the way you and your person saw the world together.

Sometimes the most healing thing you can do is let that humor keep living.

Because laughter isn't the opposite of grief.

Sometimes it's the thing that helps you breathe inside it.

The Relationship Doesn't End

One of the biggest misconceptions about loss is that the relationship ends when the person dies.

It doesn't.

Love doesn't evaporate.

The relationship simply changes form.

Grieving people continue their connection with the person they lost in quiet ways:

Talking to them.

Thinking about what they would say in certain moments.

Laughing at memories.

Telling stories about them.

Seeing pieces of them in their children, their friends, their traditions.

Shea will always be part of my life.

Not in the way I planned.

Not in the way I wanted.

But in the way love continues when someone has shaped your entire world.

Friends Sometimes Get Confused Here

When the grieving person begins functioning again, the outside world often assumes everything is fine.

People see:

The smile.

The routines returning.

The work getting done.

And they think:

They're okay now.

But functioning and healing are not the same thing.

A grieving person can rebuild a life while still carrying enormous loss.

Sometimes the most meaningful thing a friend can say — even years later — is simply:

"I still think about them."

Those words remind us that the person we lost hasn't disappeared from the world's memory.

Grief Changes You

Loss changes people.

There's no way around it.

You don't walk through something like this and come out exactly the same.

But change doesn't only mean damage.

Sometimes it means depth.

Many grieving people discover that loss reshapes their perspective in ways they never expected.

They become more compassionate.

More patient.

More aware of what truly matters.

Less tolerant of small nonsense.

More appreciative of time.

Because once you've experienced how fragile life is, you carry that awareness with you forever.

Life Expands Again — Slowly

One day you may realize something subtle but powerful:

Your life didn't end when theirs did.

It changed.

It broke.

It rearranged itself in ways you never would have chosen.

But it continues.

New memories begin forming.

New routines develop.

New experiences arrive.

Not as replacements.

Never replacements.

But *additions.*

Life expands again — slowly, carefully, imperfectly.

And somehow love continues to grow inside the life that remains.

And Maybe This Is the Point

Grief doesn't disappear.

It becomes part of the landscape.

Something you carry as you keep walking forward.

The love stays.

The memories stay.

The missing stays.

But so does life.

And the people who continue walking beside the grieving person — months later, years later — become part of that life too.

You don't need to fix grief.

You just need to stay present alongside it.

Because even after unimaginable loss, something remarkable still happens:

Life continues.

Love continues.

And the human heart — somehow — finds room to hold both.

Epilogue

A letter to the friend who stayed,

If you're reading this, I want you to know something important.

You're already doing something right.

The fact that you picked up this book means you care. It means you saw someone in pain and decided that instead of looking away, you wanted to understand how to show up for them.

That matters more than you probably realize.

Grief is one of the loneliest experiences a human being can go through. Not just because someone we love is gone, but because the world around us doesn't always know what to do with that kind of loss.

People freeze.

People panic.

People worry they'll say the wrong thing.

So sometimes they say nothing at all.

But you didn't choose nothing.

You chose curiosity.

You chose compassion.

You chose courage in the face of discomfort.

And that makes you the kind of friend every grieving person needs.

Throughout this book I've talked a lot about awkwardness, about the fear of saying the wrong thing, about the strange and unpredictable landscape of grief. If there's one thing I hope you take away from all of it, it's this:

Your presence matters more than your words.

You don't have to fix grief.

You don't have to understand every part of it.

You don't have to deliver the perfect sentence at the perfect moment.

You just have to stay.

Stay when it's uncomfortable.

Stay when you don't know what to say.

Stay when months have passed and the rest of the world has moved on.

Stay when the grieving person laughs again.

Stay when they cry again.

Just stay.

Because the friends who keep showing up—the ones who keep sending the text, making the call, inviting the walk, remembering the anniversary—those are the people who quietly help rebuild a life.

You may never see the full impact of your kindness.

But I promise you this: it matters.

More than the grieving person will ever be able to explain.

Losing Shea changed my life forever.

There will always be a space beside me where he should be. There will always be moments when I wish I could turn to him and say, "Did you see that?" or "You're not going to believe what just happened."

But there will also always be gratitude.

Gratitude for the people who stood beside me when my world fell apart.

Gratitude for the friends who didn't disappear when things got awkward.

Gratitude for the people who said, "I don't know what to say, but I'm here."

And gratitude for the strangers, acquaintances, coworkers, neighbors, and community members who chose kindness when it would have been easier to look away.

If you are someone who has shown up for a grieving friend— thank you.

You are part of the reason they are still standing.

And if you are someone reading this because you want to be that kind of friend, then let me leave you with the simplest advice I can offer:

Don't overthink it.

Don't wait for the perfect moment.

Don't worry about saying the perfect thing.

Just reach out.

Just show up.

Just stay.

Because grief is long.

But love—especially the love we show each other in our hardest moments—is longer.

With love—and no weirdness,

Dawn

Acknowledgments

There are no words big enough to honor the people who carried me when my world shattered, but these come straight from my heart.

To My Children

Sam and Jillian, you are the greatest things Shea and I ever created together. You are the living proof of the love, humor, and joy that built our family. You have shown strength and softness beyond your years, and you inspire me every day. I love you more than you will ever imagine.

To Shea's Family, Who Never Let Me Feel Like an Outsider

Your love, strength, humor, and presence were nothing short of extraordinary. Your support wasn't just comforting — it was lifesaving.

Colleen, Greg, Michael, Shawn and Pharanee— thank you for showing up in all the ways that mattered, in the immediate chaos, in the quiet days after, and in the many moments when I did not know how I was going to take the next step. Each of you brought something different: steadiness, laughter, perspective, presence, and the kind of care that made unbearable days feel just a little less impossible.

What means even more than I can fully explain is this: even in losing Shea, I never lost the family built around him. You have continued to love me like I belong right in the middle of all of you, and that has been one of the greatest gifts of my life.

Your fierce love, your humor, your honesty, your stories, your late nights, your ridiculousness, and the way you can somehow hold grief and laughter in the same room have carried me more than you probably realize.

To the nieces, nephews, cousins, aunts, and uncles — your love for Shea and for all of us radiated through every call, every hug, every message, every shared memory, and every quiet act of kindness. I will never forget it.

To My Family

Mom and Dad, thank you for caring for us in a thousand quiet ways — the cooking, the cleaning, the help with the kids, the constant presence. And to my brother and sister-in-law Bryan and Melanie: you dropped everything and flew to Michigan without blinking. And you've done it for months since. That kind of love is rare, and I will never take it for granted. To my extended family, near and far, thank you for the ways you showed care during such a difficult time.

To My Best Friends Since 8th Grade

Shelly, you were at my door the next morning — feeding my family, stocking my fridge, doing the things I was too paralyzed to even see.

Lisa, you jumped on a plane from Colorado and stood beside me through the viewing and the funeral, and on my sofa after everyone went home that night.

Dawn, your calls, texts, and steady loving presence carried me until I could hug you in person.

You have seen me at my best, and now at my absolute worst — and somehow loved me even deeper. Thank you for being my constants.

To My St. Mary family

To my "God Squad", my sisters in faith, Fr. Dwight and my Pig Palooza posse — thank you for supporting and loving me in the most practical, holy, and human ways possible. You showed up the day after Shea died, which tells me everything about who you are. You kept showing up with prayers, food, hugs, laughter, the "12 days of Christmas" and the kind of friendship that holds people upright when they forget how to stand. God knew exactly who I would need, and He sent you.

To My Dream Vacations Family

The outpouring of love from this network, my tribe built from it, and my incredible team was nothing short of remarkable. Being part of Dream Vacations has been one of the greatest blessings of my life. You surrounded me with compassion, encouragement, and strength when I needed it most. Thank you for lifting me in ways big and small.

To My BNI Family and "Book Club"

BNI gave me community, purpose, and connection — and from it grew my beloved "Book Club," the wine-and-laughter-filled sisterhood that anchored me when the world felt too heavy. You made sure I never felt alone, even when I tried to hide. Thank you for showing up monthly, intentionally, and with so much heart.

To My Charlotte Community

The support from our Charlotte friends was unwavering. You cheered for my kids, checked in on me, and held space for our family with a generosity I will never forget. Small towns have big hearts, and ours wrapped around us like a blanket.

To My SWAN Sisters

My SWAN gals — thank you for offering strength, grace, and solidarity in a season when I needed women who understood heartbreak and resilience on a soul level. Your compassion has been a lifeline.

To Everyone Who Reached Out

If you sent a text, a meal, a card, a gift, a hug, a prayer, a story about Shea — you carried a piece of my heart when I couldn't carry it myself. Every single gesture mattered.

Finally, to anyone who has ever been afraid to reach out to someone grieving: this book is for you. Thank you for caring enough to learn how to love better.

A One-Page Guide to Helping Your Grieving Friends Today

Do:

• Say something, even if it feels simple.
• Use their person's name.
• Check in more than once.
• Offer specific help.
• Allow silence.
• Remember important dates.
• Keep showing up after the funeral.

Don't:

• Say "Let me know if you need anything."
• Compare losses.
• Try to explain grief away.
• Disappear because you feel unsure.
• Rush healing.
• Avoid their person's name.

What matters most:

• You do not need perfect words.
• You do not need the right answer.
• You do not need to be profound.
• You just need to show up.

About the Author

Dawn Nowlan is a travel advisor, entrepreneur, and writer whose life changed forever after the sudden loss of her husband, Shea, in July 2025.

She is the owner of Nowlan Travel by Dream Vacations, a full-service travel agency she built with heart, grit, and a deep belief that meaningful experiences matter.

Deeply rooted in her local community, Dawn has long been active in leadership, service, and advocacy through local business organizations, charitable events, and community initiatives that reflect her belief in showing up for people well.

In the months following Shea's death, Dawn also founded Healing Journeys Widowed Travel Club — a safe space for widows and widowers to travel solo, but not alone, surrounded by people who understand that grief and living can exist side by side.

Known for her warmth, wit, and straight-to-the-point honesty, Dawn wrote *Don't Be Weird* as both a practical guide and a deeply personal offering: a book designed to help people show up better for grieving friends without overthinking, disappearing, or making things awkward.

She lives in Michigan with her two children and continues learning, day by day, what it means to build a meaningful life while carrying great love and great loss at the same time.

www.ingramcontent.com/pod-product-compliance
Lightning Source LLC
LaVergne TN
LVHW090522110826
845146LV00003B/948

* 9 7 9 8 9 9 5 6 8 9 2 0 1 *